One Gratifying Day

BOOK 2 THE ENCORE

James R. Fogg Jr.

WESTBOW
PRESS®
A DIVISION OF THOMAS NELSON
& ZONDERVAN

This book is a work of non-fiction. Unless otherwise noted, the author
and the publisher make no explicit guarantees as to the accuracy of
the information contained in this book and in some cases, names
of people and places have been altered to protect their privacy.

WestBow Press books may be ordered through booksellers or by contacting:

WestBow Press
A Division of Thomas Nelson & Zondervan
1663 Liberty Drive
Bloomington, IN 47403
www.westbowpress.com
844-714-3454

Interior Image Credit: James R. Fogg, Jr.

ISBN: 978-1-6642-4545-7 (sc)
ISBN: 978-1-6642-4546-4 (e)

Library of Congress Control Number: 2021919465

Print information available on the last page.

WestBow Press rev. date: 09/30/2021

Introduction

My hope is that all of you who are reading this book have already read Book #1 entitled "One Glorious Night." That book described my harrowing experience and escape during the very long night of October 18-19, 2016, while elk hunting in the high ranges of Colorado. My Higher Power came to my rescue in an event that I shall never forget; changing my life like anything I have ever experienced before. The point to be remembered in this Book #2 occurred during daylight hours, and resulted in a totally different result; "One Gratifying Day". My intension in writing this Book #2 is to be, as little as possible, repetitious of my first book, to not burden you with repeated events, as I disclosed to You my final elk hunt in 2019. As much as I tried, I found it impossible to avoid repeating a few points which I described in Book # One. I plead with You, therefore, to read the first book, "One Glorious Night" before reading this one. Who can tell? You just may catch me with a slight wavering of the facts between the two books. I was only 78 years old when I composed the first book. Now, at the ripe old age of 81, I could possibly slip up and misconstrue a fact or two. Catch me if you can!

Oops, you just caught me. Look on page 5 of my first book and you will read; (However, as I will be 79 in 2017, I may have to hang it up. Climbing those ten to eleven thousand-foot mountains in deep snow on foot is not as easy as it once was when Bill and I were in our thirties).

Thus, you know I went hunting again in October 2019, at 81 years of age. This time, I shall not go back on my word, and hunt in 2020 at 82 years old! I will just settle for the gym.

Dedication

I WOULD LIKE TO DEDICATE this book, first and foremost, to every one of my soulmates who appreciates and is stirred by the thrill of venturing out, all alone, to test their strength and skill against that formidable foe, known as "wild game", To all we hunters. You surely understand and have enjoyed the excited adrenalin rush as You first encounter the creature of your pursuit, whether it be a cotton tail rabbit, turkey, bear, or that elegant bull elk. I wish every one of you the same delightful excitement that I have experienced on so many occasions. The reward is always worth the hard work expended. The thrilling adventure is your gift to appreciate!

Additionally, I wish each one of you who strives for satisfaction in achieving your goal, whether you ever hunt or not, a profound sense of satisfaction from your worthwhile pursuits. For example, to set your goal at the gym, and often surpassing it, brings much gratification and joy to your inner soul. This is my desire that each of you reach an internal peace and tranquility that makes life so very rewarding. Work and play diligently and your body will reward you with peace.

For any of you who are not blessed with these benefits due to health conditions, God loves you and I love you. Please always keep your chin up. There is room in this World for all God's children. Bless you all!

Acknowledgments

WHEN I CONTEMPLATE ALL THESE 47 safe and fruitful years of Colorado's high mountain adventures with my closest relatives and dearest friends, I cannot help feeling my deep appreciation for their companionship. They were each very special. Our fortunate successes were a direct result of our desire, determination, and cooperation between all members of our hunting camp. We were definitely a fraternity of brothers bonded by our appreciation and respect for one another. All for one and one for all! Now that I am left all alone, among our original group, I feel so blessed that we traversed those high peaks without any serious injuries, always pulling for each other's blessed successes. I loved every one of them and surely miss them. My Lord has brought them all safely home.

Now, I pay homage to our equally talented brothers

that comprise our camp today; members that will joyfully carry on our tradition into the distant future. They are all descendants and close friends of our original camp members. I impart them all my complete respect and blessing as they "carry on an old family tradition", as Hank Jr. would croon!

However, none of this would ever have been possible without the constant guidance and direct help from our ever loving God, through Jesus Christ, our Savior. You can see that my 2016 experience has altered my life in a profound way!

Forward

IN MY FIRST BOOK, " One Glorious Night", I disclosed to you the perilous journey, which I endured, and survived, with the never ending guidance of my Lord; an experience that I shall never forget, nor fail to appreciate.

MY intention was to let this book stand on it's own merit, and not add another. However, at the age of 81 and feeling pretty spry, I decided to go elk hunting once again to test my endurance and skill against that formidable foe. Now, I am so very pleased that I ventured back into the high mountain country of Colorado, and was rewarded for my effort. Bull elk #25 for me (24 already recorded) was awaiting my arrival but only the Lord knew it. Neither that bull nor I ever suspected our chance meeting on that late afternoon of Oct.12,2019, much to his chagrin. It was the opening day of the season, and the elk were not alarmed. Only one shot up above was heard at about five PM. It was, as it turned out, from the gun of my young pal, Triston Berringer, dropping bull elk # 119 from our camp. Subsequently, after reaching my goal of #25, my appetite for climbing those high peaks to hunt those Royal Bulls has finally ended!

I could never surpass the thrill of my last two hunts (October 2016, October 2019). Thus, my commitment has subsided and my contentment is complete. Let the Youth take charge, and report their exciting experiences to me. I wish them all the best of success and happiness in the future. I'll just enjoy my time in my garden, growing veggies and flowers. My Church and Gym still holds a lot of my time. Also, my five Grandchildren and their parents are eager for my attention and I am willing to give it! May God bless them all.

Book #2
"One Gratifying Day"

IF IT'S OCTOBER IN THE Colorado Rockies, the leaves must fall, the snows will come, we hunters head for the hills, and the elk become nervous and very cautious. See those same elk in June and July when the grass is green and abundant, and you will not find them alert and on guard. You will discover them as I have done many times in summer months, lying at total peace on the hillside, as they fatten up from the previous snowy winter. I have observed fifty to sixty adult elk lying down, very relaxed, in a quite open quaking aspen forest.

While the adults are so very peaceably at rest, their many young calves are running all about having fun. They don't know what to do with all of their energy. They seem to be playing a game of tag. What I believe they are actually doing, in addition to exercising and strengthening their young bodies (as you and I did when we were young) is also sizing up their playmates. They are learning at such a young age just which will someday be the dominate cow, and more importantly, which will someday be the "Herd Bull" as he fights off all competition in building his harem of cows. Really, dominance is the name of this playful summer game.

After such strenuous exercise, these young calves do not need grass for lunch; just run over to their moms and make them get up, so they can have their fill of milk. The entire herd knows there is absolutely no threat from their enemies. Not even a family of coyotes concern the herd since the large bulls with lethal horns could dispatch them easily if they could only catch them. The occasional encounter with a bear or a mountain lion, or a rare pack of wolves could be bothersome, but the elk herd will just run away to hopeful security.

However, there is one mortal enemy that is craftier than the rest; who uses instruments to his advantage. He is man! Thank goodness for the elk. He is only allowed to pursue them for five weeks each year. Elk know the seasons of the year just as surely as we people do. They know when to hone their skills.

Other than these dangers, an elk's life is one of full freedom and enjoyment which would make our domesticated cattle very envious, if they could compare lifestyles. An elk's life consists of exercising, eating, and multiplying. What a blessed existence, except they must use caution in the fall. Additionally, the cold winter snows do often cause them hardship.

Do you wonder how elk can fatten up by lying still and relaxing on the hillside? Shouldn't they be busy, out in the meadow, eating grass? No, they did that last night. What? Yes, the elk (and also moose) can do that because they are of the "Bovine" family. Just like your domesticated cattle. That means they can chew their "cud", a term given to those special animals with two stomachs. Really!?; animals with two stomachs? Absolutely, those Bovines are unique.

Just study our friendly cattle in the heat of the day, and you will witness them relaxing under the shade of the trees, casually chewing their "cud". This means they filled their first stomach to capacity in the cool of the morning. Then, later in the day, they will lie down or stand while they regurgitate their fodder from their first stomach and chew (grind) it into succulent nourishment to be passed back down into their second stomach for full digestion, into energy and fat.

Elk exercise the very same system as our tame cattle do, but with a much different feeding time frame. Cattle know that we are their friends. They trust us. Elk do not, and who can blame them? You will not find elk out grazing in the mountain meadows, except on rare occasions, during daylight hours. They feed during the dark of night; then retreat to the deep forest by dawn to relax, sleep, and grind their fodder into a usable energy source.

No longer will a large elk herd lie around half asleep in the open Quaking Aspens. These beautiful Aspen trees are so named "Quakes" because their delicate leaves tremble in the slightest breeze. We hunters just call them "Quakes", (pronounced "Quakies"), instead of Aspens.

The mountain ridge just west of our camp is known as "Quake Ridge" because of its abundance of Aspens. Believe me, an elk herd can trespass through that Aspen forest at near lightning speed when startled.

I once stood stone still one early morning and watched a giant herd rushing past within twenty yards of me, dashing toward their very tangled sanctuary of the deep timber. There was no possibility of counting them as they were running five and six abreast. They were dashing from the huge meadow below after daylight had caught them still feeding. They must have seen hunters approaching and became much alarmed. Though it was hunting season, I did not raise my gun. I only stood in awe and marveled at the largest herd I had ever seen. I made no attempt to shoot, because at their speed and quantity, I was afraid of accidentally hitting a cow or young bull, which are both illegal to shoot. Therefore, I remained motionless as they sped by. Almost none of them sensed my presence.

An interesting mishap occurred as the huge herd was speeding past me. One or more elk on my side (the left side of the fleeing herd) saw me and veered to their right to avoid me. This quick maneuvering pushed a cow on the right side of the running herd to slam head first into a giant Aspen tree, which knocked her unconscious. The massive herd kept on speeding by leaving her prone and all alone after their departure. Not wanting to cause her any more fright, I stood there watching but very still. After two or three minutes she awoke, lifter her head to look around while still dazed. I could tell when she saw me, because she quickly tried to regain her footing, but to no avail for a couple more minutes. She finally succeeded in standing and slowly walking away. I said not one word, nor made any movement. I figured she had experienced enough trauma for one day. I felt sorry for her.

As I was departing my hunting land at season's end, I found a local Colorado game and fish commission agent and told him of my experience. He said to me, "Do you know how many elk were in that herd?" I told him I had no idea; just a multitude of elk. He told me there were over 200 in that herd. I asked him how did he know? He said; because he had counted them just at first daylight as they were still meandering in the very large meadow below Quake Ridge.

No, there is not a shortage of elk in Colorado. If you would like one, then you must first get into good shape, work very, very hard and be ultra-knowledgeable and lucky if you ever wish to have success. I hunt them, but I love watching them and respect them greatly. They are definitely my favorite of all wild animals. Therefore, I pay a large sum of money each year to assist them through severe winter months. If you hunt elk in Colorado and live out of state, you clearly catch my drift. However, Colorado big game officials do provide excellent care by feeding the herds in severe weather. They are good people.

Now, how about those poor mule deer? They, having one stomach, are not of the Bovine family. That is why deer are identified as bucks, does, and fawns. Elk, just like you domesticated cattle, are called bulls, cows, and calves.

Deer, as opposed to elk. Would starve during the winter if they behaved as elk do. Deer, with only one stomach, must eat the high energy foods in the forest, like bush and tree buds, to survive the severe winter weather. Sure, you may see white-tail deer out eating grass, especially in eastern U.S., in warmer climates, but even here they gather high energy food from the woods. For that reason, deer meat (venison) has a wild taste as elk does not. In other words, you are what you eat! Because of that fact, I do not hunt deer; I do not eat venison. I could easily shoot deer or turkeys from my back porch, but they are safe. Why do harm to "Bambi" or my friendly turkeys? I feed them daily in the spring time. Do you see? We vicious mean hunters have a heart after all. We consume our elk, while most of you, other than vegetarians, joyfully eat your beef from that cow which never had a chance. They lived out their lives without freedom. How is that for turning the tables?

Now, back to those sly, crafty creatures; those elk. As the autumn temperature drops those elk change their habits. They must deploy a much different system if they wish to grow old and gray. There will be no more peaceful resting in the semi open Quakes. Instead, they will spend all day resting and sleeping in the thick timber where the advantage goes to them. Here, a hunter has all the disadvantages. The hunter will almost certainly be seen, heard, or smelled as we labor to crawl over, under, or walk around the constant thick mat of downed, dead trees which have fallen in recent years, giving away our presence. Yes, we do smell awful to elk, and they don't like it. However, that odor works both ways. I can always smell a giant bull if he is upwind from me. During the Rut, those bulls enjoy a roll in their bogs. They intentionally urinate in those wet bogs; then wallow profusely in them to obtain a strong scent of masculinity to excite the cows. Unfortunately for them, I can certainly smell them strongly whenever I pass by downwind from them. On one early morning, as I was climbing alone in the darkness, I was startled by a strong bull odor, which told me where he was; definitely upwind. I continued my climb but decided to choose my morning stand in the first of two large meadows, instead of choosing my oft used top meadow. At about 10:30 Am here comes three cows followed by a huge six by six pointer, cutting across this lower meadow, heading for the extremely dense, downed timber for their daily refuge. He quickly became my second Royal Bull Elk. If I had chosen my usually preferred top stand that morning, those four elk would have passed below me, completely out of view.

An elk's eyesight is reputed to be seven times that of man. Their hearing is far superior to ours.

Elk will usually post a guard to alert the herd if an intruder with gun in hand is approaching. I have attempted this maneuver so many times, only to be discovered by the herd and then left all alone, very tired and scratched from thorns, etc. as they fled. It is disheartening.

With all those advantages going to the elk, how does a poor hunter stand a chance of feeding his family? Colorado game and fish report that, on average, only one of every ten hunters going after a bull will have success.

With the elk holding the Trump card, how can a hunter be lucky enough to bag a bull, when they know all the tricks? Patience, patience, patience!

A hunter's best chance of success is to think like the elk. Study all their habits, then position one's self between their food source (meadow) and their deep timber resting place where they spend each day. Most elk are shot during the first hour of daylight as the herd is returning from feeding; heading back to their protective cover, and the last hour before darkness as they leave their safe refuge; heading down to their favorite mountain meadow to feed. To accomplish this feat, elk will form several trails. A skilled hunter must study those trails to discover their recent usage, either by tracks or droppings. Also study young trees along their routes to discern if big bulls have recently rubbed the bark from the tree trunks, as they remove the velvet from their horns and sharpened them.

Then I position myself in view of that trail, wait patiently, and don't move or make any sound. My favorite is when I can view two or three crossing trails from one position. My chances will go up as I view more trails, as elk can often be so unpredictable.

Choosing my stand (hiding place) is of utmost importance since elk can smell us instantly if we are upwind of them, and be gone in a flash. Remember, we stink! Elk cannot stand the smell of soap. So, get downwind from their trails and be motionless, but ultra-alert of any sound or motion. What is very frustrating is when the wind keeps shifting directions to alert the herd.

Please notice that I said "herd" because elk rarely travel alone. An elk herd will always be led by an old, very smart, and cautious lead cow. She, being old, very experienced and super alert without a young calf to care about, is only concerned with guiding all her friends to safety. Additionally, she is super cautious if there is that giant bull trailing back at or near the rear of that herd.

No elk herd will ever be led by a bull since he is half crazy during the "Rut" – mating season. He would lead his harem into total destruction since his concentration is only absorbed with his desires. Just the same, when it's his turn to cross a meadow, he will do so with semi-flight speed usually. Whenever I see a herd moving down a trail, I am like a statue, observing every member that passes with my gun at the super-ready. Finally, the giant fellow, the pride of the herd, will appear. He is mine! Then I take off my coat, roll up my sleeves, get out my saw and knives, and spend very hard labor for the next four hours. Didn't I tell you that elk hunting is not for the timid?

I can usually tell if a Big Bull is in her herd. She, the lead cow, seems more cautious than ever. When she does step out into the open and begin grazing, she seems more nervous than usual, and will very frequently look back to where she entered the clearing. Her biggest concern is that bull. That is my tipoff that he will eventually come into the clearing after more cows come out. Don't try tricking me, Mister Big Bull, I'll just bide my time and wait for you.

Now, I shall divulge a secret that I have kept form you "Road Hunters" for all these years. The greatest advantage any elk hunter can have is to travel for miles from the nearest road; then camp and hunt where the elk live. They don't seem to mind just as long as you are very quiet, out of sight, and down wind. True, the herd will wander over a twenty-five square mile area. The trick is to locate the herd without spooking them. Then decide, every day, where you will set up your ambush location for that afternoon and for the next morning's hunt. As the herd moves, you move also.

Our camp is four miles from the nearest road and sits at 9,400 feet of altitude. We hunt up to 11,300 feet high and up to eight miles from the nearest road. That kind of hunting is not for the faint of heart.

To have the greatest success, never start a fire or eat breakfast in the morning. Eat your sandwich and snacks, packed the night before, around eleven A.M. if all is quiet, without any elk company. If elk are present, hold off the eating. You can eat tomorrow! This elk hunting is serious business. From one until two P.M. is generally a great time to eat lunch since the elk are usually asleep. But get ready early, and choose your afternoon stand according to recent elk activity, and nestle down very still from 4 P.M. until near dark. Now have patience and don't give up.

We have been fortunate through the years. As of about four months ago we have harvested a total of 121 bull elk; never a cow nor calf. Those we don't want. We only crave the huge dominant fellows with big racks on their heads. In Colorado, only bulls with at least four points on a side can be taken. All other bulls are illegal. We crave the 5 & 6 pointers; (5 or 6 per side) but sometimes settle for a four pointer, if the season is getting late. Old elk can grow 7 points per side, but that is rare. I've never seen one while hunting. They are called "Imperials." Six pointers are known as "Royals." We have brought home several of those.

Enough about tactics. I wish now to disclose many of our hunters involved during all these forty- seven years, and close by telling of my final elk hunt just three months ago – Oct. 12 through Oct. 16, 2019.

Nothing ever remains the same. Our camp has changed membership through the years as we founders depart and hand the reins over to our capable and dedicated next generation and their children and very close friends. After counting, by memory, every member of our camp through all these years from 1972 until the present time, I come up with 22 hunters, but I may be forgetting one or two. However, we have never had more than eight in camp at any one time; often only five or six. When Bill and I founded this camp, there were only two of us. Within a year we increased our membership to seven.

My best buddy and hunting camp cofounder, Bill Berringer, and I first met at McGuire Air Force Base in late March 1968. That was after my return from one year as a pilot in Vietnam, where I flew 146 combat missions.

Bill and his wife, Judy, became fast friends with my wife, Mary Lou and I, as we moved only fifty yards away from them in "On Base Housing." We had no children yet, but Bill and Judy had two; a daughter named Robyn and a son, Todd. Their third child, Brett would come along later. By then, we had a son, Randy, and a daughter, Robyn. Also, by then Bill and I had both left the active Air Force and became pilots for Western Airlines, living in the Los Angeles, California area.

Not wanting to break all ties with the Military, and needing extra income for our families, we both joined the Air Force Reserves for the next four years. Also, the Vietnam war was raging as hot as ever; dedication for us still persisted.

Bill and I, while still flying for Western Airlines, soon were elevated to Aircraft Commanders (Pilots) in the U.S. Air Force Reserves at Norton Air Force Base, San Bernardino, California. We were in the same squadron again, flying the giant C-141 Star-lifter.

Back to Vietnam we went, resupplying our fighting forces. We were usually loaded with all types of war material, but often transported fresh troops for combat duty. On our trip home, we were often loaded with joyful troops as their tours had ended. Some were not so joyful as they were bandaged from various wounds, coming back to the states for hospital stays. Sad to say, many were not even this lucky. Very often, our huge plane cabins were loaded with caskets stacked all the way up to the ceiling, from front to rear. Very sad relatives would be awaiting their arrival. Enough, already, of these gloomy details. Let's hit a more pleasant note and get back to hunting elk.

Through all this turmoil of holding two jobs and keeping our families happy, Bill and I so very often discussed what it would be like to down one of those giant bull elk. We both had hunted most of our mature lives, after deer, antelope, turkey, and pheasants, but we considered elk to be the grand prize.

Just as soon as conditions permitted, we joyfully departed Los Angeles (LAX) and moved to Denver, Colorado, still flying for Western Airlines and the USAF reserves. Here, we could live out our long lingering dream of pursuing those mysterious Wapiti (elk) that inhabited the high ranges of the Colorado Rockies.

With both of our families firmly planted in Colorado in 1972 we encouraged Bill's father, Mr. Berringer, his brother, Warren, his brother-in-law, J.B. McClure, and Bill's uncle and cousin to go hunting with us above Rabbit Ears Pass. On the first day, none of us saw anything. But, just as darkness fell, I definitely heard sticks breaking as a herd was settling in for the night, quite close to my stand, a log that I was sitting on. I very silently left my stand and departed down and around that knoll and crept back to camp for the night. I sort of confessed to my campmates that evening that I was going to down a big bull on the following morning which drew a hearty, teasing laugh from one and all. I withstood the ribbing as I pondered my strategy for the following morning. Before daylight of the next morning, I was again sitting all alone on that same log; very quiet, intensely listening, but I heard nothing. At about 10:15 AM, a very wise and old Lead Cow stepped out into the meadow by my stand, only forty yards away. I watched as 43 more cows and calves crossed that meadow in plain view, but no bull crossed after them. That is strange, I thought, because a herd that large would certainly have a huge bull lurking at or near the rear of the herd, but none appeared at 10:15AM or eleven o'clock. At around 11:30, was I ever shocked to see the largest bull I have ever seen, with a giant rack, suddenly burst across that meadow about three hundred yards uphill, just inside of the other side of the clearing, and stop to look around at his surroundings. I put my scope on him and was about to shoot when he quickly departed into the timber. I was immediately saddened for not shooting sooner, though 300 yards is a long shot and requires time for accuracy. I had waited for an instant too long, I mused, but my sadness would not last long. Someone in the timber, on the far side of the meadow startled him, resulting in my shock at hearing him dashing through the trees, breaking some lower dead branches, as he sped straight toward me! He burst into my meadow about 120 yards away, angling to the very spot where the 44 cows and calves had first appeared almost two hours before. I brought him down only briefly with my first shot, just as he was jumping the small stream that ran lengthwise down this meadow. Before he could reach my side of this meadow, I shot him twice more. This was obvious to me because I could clearly see the three holes in his side, looking like a triangle as he continued to my side of the clearing, and stood looking around at where his enemy was. Very excitedly, I jumped out into the opening, with both of us facing each other. He glared at me for only a second before he quickly turned and started to jump over a large log about four feet above the ground. At that moment I made one final shot that probably saved my life! In all the excitement I ran quickly to where he had fallen, just inside of the trees. That huge Bull suddenly rose up from the ground with his massive, seventeen inch long, brow tines, that makes all of my brow tines from other (even Royal Bulls) seem like dwarfs. Believe me, I have measured them still on the wall in my office. Joe Jonas, the taxidermist in Denver who mounted him told me that this bull's rack was the largest (5 by 5) rack that he had ever seen. I received 510 pounds of elk meat from the butcher, which far outweighs any other bull I have ever shot! With his brow tines threateningly near my stomach, (the rest of his massive rack towered far above my head), he bellowed at me with his frightful sounds. Our eyes were no more than three feet apart as he stared at me with unbelievable fierce anger, and I peered back at him in total surprise, unable to move in my sudden state of shock. Once again, I needed help from Above, and it was delivered at just the right moment, thank Heavens. God is great! That last shot which I delivered just as he was jumping that tall log, penetrated his spine above his rear hips, paralyzing both of his rear legs. He could only rise on his front legs and thus couldn't give the thrust he desired to drive those beautiful brow tines through me. He would have tossed me over his head and finished my life at his ease and pleasure if only he could have stood on all fours. I froze in disbelief and terror for one or two minutes, which seemed so much longer as I awaited his plunge! Suddenly, to my relief, I noticed his life faltering as he stopped roaring at me and glaring so fiercely. He was weakening fast and became very quiet, to my amazement and relief. He collapsed and tumbled to the ground with his nose landing only inches from my feet and died, with me standing there like in a trance! But I shall remember that moment for the rest of my life. I would never pull that stupid trick again. Ever after, I would slowly walk up in front of a supposed dead bull with my gun at the ready at about twenty yards distance and stare at his eyes to discern if there is any life left. Then I slowly walk around to his rear and give him a swift kick. If there is no motion, then I prepare myself for four hours of hard labor; it's skinning time. He was the largest elk we ever shot among our 121 now. Although Bill, Todd, and Brett Berringer have also bagged some massive bulls.

About five minutes after this close call, an old man (mind You, about seventy years old) rode up on his horse with his rifle stashed in his holster, and asked, "Did you get one"? I was speechless, and could only point to the bull lying just inside the timber. He understood and rode his horse around for a clear view. He was shocked, and said to me "My Lord, I guess you did get one". I tried to converse with him, but I could not because my body was shaking so severely and my teeth were chattering. I attempted to apologize for my pathetic speech, but he soothed me somewhat when he stated, " No need to apologize son; I've been hunting these elk most all of my life, and I still go all to pieces when I get one anywhere near this big" I tried to thank him as I was trying to hold my jaw shut with both hands to prevent their chattering!

Within ten minutes, all of my campmates arrived on the scene, after hearing what sounded like a small war breaking out, and figured it was me. They were no longer laughing and teasing me, like the night before. They didn't say it, but probably were thinking," it would have been nice if Jim had been more descriptive the previous evening about his suspicions of elk activity near his stand". I had now proved my point; "Don't laugh at poor old Jim Fogg when he gives you a clue". Anyway, they all forgave me and helped me skin out my elk. We all seven divided up the meat, which became standard from that day forward.

Though successful with one bull in 1972, trekking seven miles into the timber was stressful. We began to search for a more rewarding hunting area. After careful research, Bill and I decided to try our luck in Routt National Forest; actually, in the hills above a huge meadow known as Bunker Basin. The primary ridge known as Main Ridge climbs all the way up to Pyramid Peak (over 12,000 feet). I shall not repeat the particulars of our fortunate move, since I do not want to impart the same news twice. I shared it all in Book #1 – One Glorious Night; remember it? In order to hunt this wilderness area in the fall of 1973, Bill and I went scouting the entire area in July of that year, three months before elk season, to decide where to place our camp in October. We were highly impressed with this entire wilderness area, including a large herd of elk we encountered in the heart of Bunker Basin. This area will be our Utopia.

However, we still needed to find a way to pack into our chosen campsite, and where to leave our pickups while hunting. Again, fortune smiled down on us.

We discovered to our delight, a man named Pat Mantle, who moved his base of operations from Steamboat Springs locale to this Bunker Creek area each year to prepare for the onslaught of elk hunters from several states that would require his services, come hunting season. Everyone in that area knew him as a valuable outfitter with the largest herd of horses in Colorado. Pat used many of these horses to transport hunters and all supplies to their appointed campsites. During elk season, his many guides would do everything for a hunter except shoot his bull. Then his guides would come and pack out the hunter's bull, if he was successful, plus all of his camping gear. To Bill and I, that was not elk hunting. We refused to be spoon fed.

Pat Mantle was a renowned character with a direct but pleasant personality; Bill and I sought him out because we didn't want to infringe on any one of his chosen campsites and build an enemy. Lucky for us, our chosen campsite, way back into the timber, was separate from all of Pat's; thus, no conflict there.

Once we discovered him, Bill and I quickly formed a bond with Pat. We knew we would gain from his knowledge of Bunker Basin. Also, we could gain from his provisions such as horses to hire, if ever needed. We were self- sufficient since we owned and brought our treasured donkey, Buford, with us. He, plus all of our heavy backpacks would take everything into camp that we needed for the hunt. Also, he would haul out all the elk that we would be fortunate to get, carefully packed in the paniers on each side of his pack saddle. Later, we would add three more donkeys to our herd, all offspring of Buford's. They were all three very beneficial, but Buford was king. We even named our favorite meadow near the top of the mountain after him; Buford's Meadow, because of the quantity of elk carcasses he hauled from there. In recent years after Buford's death from old age, we do hire horses from Pat Mantle's camp.

Now, it's time to make his acquaintance. We drove our pickup into his base camp area and introduced ourselves. Pat seemed quite friendly. Apparently, he respected our spunk, drive, and determination at hunting elk.

I shall never forget that first conversation with Pat as he attempted to add us to his "packing customers" that coming fall. After explaining our game plan for our hunt,

Pat wished us both the greatest success, but added; "If you two have never hunted elk before, you will need one of my guides to assist you. Otherwise, you two 'dudes' will never be successful." But with our usual determination, we both thanked Pat, and said we would take our chances. However, we never went hunting without dropping by to visit Pat before and after our hunt. We never had to tell Pat of our successes. His many guides would discover our transportation of big bulls, along with our camp gear at closure of every hunt. We still would drop by to pay our respects and often have a beer with Pat.

After years of very successful hunting, Pat wanted to hire us as his guides. We thanked him and said we preferred our current system. Pat was our buddy up until his Earthly departure many years later. We still refer to his outfit as "that Pat Mantle camp."

Sad to say, "Father Time" has taken a toll on our original "Band of Brothers." Of our original hunting group, only I have survived.

Our oldest member, Mr. Berringer, (Bill's dad) hunted with us for years, marking the first of four generations of Berringers in our same camp. He was a definite joy to be around. I adored his personality and humor. His inexhaustible supply of jokes kept our camp laughing at night. Rumor persists that I also assisted him in joke telling. Mister Berringer hunted with us until the age of

74 years old. We all marveled at how anyone could still climb those steep hills at that age. Who could guess that years later, one addicted old elk hunter, myself, would be climbing them at 81 years of age. Mr. Berringer departed for Glory years ago after viewing with much satisfaction the accomplishments of his and his wife's decedents. His darling wife, Mrs. Lois Berringer, joined him many years later at the ripe old age of 96 years of pleasant earthly life, but endured sad times of losing many of her most prized family members. Of her four children, she outlived three of them.

Bill's twin brother, Warren, hunted with us for years and was a great friend. However, Warren succumbed to cancer far too early in life. Our visits to his hospital bed were depressing to all of us.

We had high hopes for Warren's son, Brook, to join us hunting elk as soon as his football days were over. Brook, #18, quarterback on that famous Nebraska football team that won the National Championship by defeated the University of Miami in the Orange Bowl. Almost all his relatives and close friends were there including my wife and I, to witness the event. I shall never forget his calm demeanor as he sat so comfortably relaxed as he chatted with all of us just hours before the game.

It appeared that we would have to wait a few years, as several Pro football teams were after him. We were all very shocked and saddened at the news, as the Grim Reaper stepped in to cancel all future plans for him.

Brook and his fiancé's brother were flying a piper cub airplane on a windy, gusty morning and climbed to around three hundred feet. Suddenly the plane stalled, and drove into the ground at near vertical attitude. Brook's proud and loving mom, Jan, and his two sisters will never get over that tragedy. I still am very saddened when I think of his loss. We all adored him. His funeral was very gloomy and shocking as Coach Osborn, and all Brook's coaches spoke of his extraordinary talent and gripping personality. The Pros were waiting but the Lord brought him home.

My friendship Brother Bill, after all these years of family gathering, Air Force and Airline experiences, and so very many elk hunt exciting adventures, contracted lymphatic cancer, which took him to our Lord in April, 2013, as I stated in my first book. His two sons, Todd and Brett, and I spoke at Bill's funeral. Our two families were so very close.

Speaking of our two families, you may recall from book #1 that Bill "was" my brother. Also, I stated that Bill's wife, Judy, and my wife Mary Lou, "are" sisters. Sadly, Judy, passed only three months after my 2016 debacle, and went to join Bill in Paradise.

My close pal from Virginia Tech and elk hunting buddy for years, Poss Horton, passed away in April of 2014. We had been very close friends ever since we both turned 18 and were in the same squadron in college. Poss was only twelve days younger than I – birth of August 4th versus August 16th, 1938.

Poss told me, from his hospital bed, the week before he passed, that he was always very sure that I would die first. He said that I had always taken so very many risky chances with my life, such as volunteering for a war when I didn't have to attend. Poss told me, in front of his wife, Saundra, on one side of his bed and I on the other, that it just wasn't fair for him to die before me. We all three laughed in a distressed way. One week later, I gave the eulogy at his funeral up in Northern Virginia.

Bill's brother-in-law, J.B. McClure, who hunted with us for most of our many years, and provided for all four of our donkeys near his home in Goodland, Kansas, passed away just last year, and left another hole in my heart. I greatly cherished his friendship. J.B. was special. Just like the rest of us, he was blessed with a wonderful loving family. His wife, Judith, is the only remaining child of Mr. & Mrs. Berringer, having lost Dianne (their oldest), Warren, and William, known to us as Bill.

Of our original group, now only I survive. How, many of my friends do question, since I have taken so many chances and somehow pulled through? From combat and a multitude of mishaps, like being lost in a high mountain snowstorm, falls from tall ladders, and scrapes along the way, my journey, so many times has been life threatening.

Whenever I reflect on my life, I am reminded of a famous boxer who wrote a book about his life, in and out of the ring, published in 1954. He was the champion prize fighter, Rocky Graziano. In his book, Rocky recounts his life, which its title; "Somebody Up There Likes Me: The Story of My Life So Far", gives us a quick glimpse of his life as we glean from its cover. Though my conscience, temperament, and talent could never equal that of Rocky, I feel the same sentiment as I plow through the winter of my life. Somebody up there surely likes me, as I saw so very clearly during my many hours in the snowy blizzard, while hunting elk in October of 2016 – Book #1.

One thing I do know absolutely! I am still here because my God, and my Savior, Jesus Christ, have never given up on me, bringing me through all perils and hardships safely. Why, exactly, I do not know for certain. My wife reminds me often that my Lord is using me, now and in the future, to influence others to live a more gratifying, rewarding, and righteous life. If so, then praise the Lord, let it be. According to her, my life's experience can influence others and convince them to never give up on life. Just over that hill is a brighter future, a glorious one even.

Far from being anything resembling a Saint, I have always tried to live an honest and fruitful life. My biggest problem has always been my uncontrollable vigor. Also, my temper has occasionally disturbed me and others, but I try diligently to improve. Older age has helped.

My consumption of strong spirits ceased many, many years ago. One thing is certain. Bill and I have never allowed alcohol in our camp. The younger generation still carries on this tradition.

Who is this younger generation? Well many that hunted with us years ago are alive and well, as they and their families prosper.

There are others who hunted with us and apparently lost their desire. Also, very often, family life obligations interfered, preventing their long absence from home. Raising children with their academics, and various sport activities, is a full-time job these days. For example, J.B.'S son, Mike, hunted with us for years when he was single. Then he got married.

My son, Randy, and son-in-law, Kevin have both hunted elk with me across those ridges many years ago, but not anymore. Truth is that neither Randy nor Kevin contracted elk hunting fever as severely as I did. They don't understand the pleasure of prowling or sitting, very still, all alone, atop high mountain peaks in sub- freezing weather, in deep snow.

Call me crazy, but I have considered every hunt an extremely exciting adventure, and will bet that those Berringers feel the same way.

However, it seems never too cold or miserable for my son Randy and his family to ski (snowboard actually) for days at a time down Colorado's many slopes, especially Steam Boat Springs. To each his own, I suppose. I once went with them but not now; old age has crept in. Randy, Robyn, and I had great fun skiing (in and often out of bounds) many years ago. We had season passes.

Both Randy and Kevin are airline pilots. Randy flies the Airbus A-320 and 321 for Spirit Airlines. Kevin is a captain for Delta Airlines here in Atlanta. I retired from Delta Airlines as a captain in 1998. Bill Berringer followed suit in 2001.

Kevin bought a plane and is now teaching his two sons to fly. He just can't help it. Kevin is "just carrying on an old family tradition" as Hank Junior was prone to croon about his famous father. Kevin and Robyn's oldest son, Jake, is now a freshman at Auburn University, majoring in Aviation, Professional Flight, with all intentions on joining Delta Airlines, Just alike his father and grandfather before him.

So, who are the current leaders and members of this traditional brotherhood of hunters? The two leaders are brothers; Todd and Brett Berringer. They are the grandsons of Mr. Berringer. Bill's father. We could not have left our camp to better leaders than those two. Both are extremely dedicated and very successful hunters as well as camp organizers. Successful elk hunting requires hard work; careful planning and execution. They both are fully up to the challenge.

Todd and Brett were both hired by United Airlines as pilots; thus, carrying on our name, "that airline camp" as other camps refer to us. Todd has remained with United for over 20 years, but Brett has been on military leave, flying for the Colorado Air Guard for nearly 20 years, flying the F-16 Fighter Jet. Brett is currently a Lieutenant Colonel who has served his unit on several extended missions to danger zones around the Earth.

Among Brett's military accomplishments are four deployments to war zones in defense of our Great Republic. He has served three tours identified as "Iraqi Freedom" and one combat deployment to Afghanistan, known as "Operation Resolute Support." Brett and his unit have constantly been on alert, ever since 9-11. Brett Berringer is a warrior! He will retire from the military this coming Oct. 1st and spend the rest of his aviation career as a United Pilot, just as his older brother, Todd, has done. Both of them will fly out of Denver, their "home" town. We Delta folks live near that other "home" town, Atlanta.

Brett will retain his original seniority number at United which means everything to airline pilots.

The two brothers, Todd and Brett are close knit. They have never had a disagreement in my presence. Todd, being the older brother, assumes the role of the enforcer if our camp is ever infringed upon by outsiders.

Todd and I have always been very great friends, but both of us have known for many years that we must be careful. We are too much alike. I sometimes have mild difficulty getting along with anyone who is just like me. Opposites attract! Todd's dad, Bill, as dear friends as we were, and I could sometimes have strong disagreements, especially if we were tired and hungry from a long day of hunting and seeing no elk. It was difficult at times having two "Herd Bulls" in the same camp. Now here comes Todd! Three of those bulls, at times, was quite challenging.

Also competing bulls are one thing. Striving airline captains are another, but at the same time could be similar as I look back on it. "You must be careful now, because I am the Boss." As the old airline joke went; "You can always tell a captain, but you can't tell him much!" somehow, we all remained great friends for all those years without hurting one another. Praise the lord.

Brett, on the other hand, though just as strong in personality as we three, is more of a diplomat; a "cooperate and graduate" type of man; I firmly believe Brett inherited this benevolent trait from his mother, Judy. My Mary Lou and I have agreed since we first met her that she was one of the kindest, sweetest, and most pleasant persons you will ever encounter. "The apple never falls far from the tree." Brett picked up her qualities which makes him a joy to be around. Brett and Todd's dad, Bill, brought the strength, drive, and determination to the family. Their mom, Judy, brought the loving kindness and peace to the family. That is why their children and grandchildren are so blessed. Brett surely has her genes, which I believe accounts for our bond. His and my personalities mesh nearly to perfection.

For example, we were in a friendly discussion about four years ago, when Brett shocked me with delight. He said, to the best of my recollection, these words. "Jim, when I started hunting here at the age of fourteen, I knew nothing but rumor about elk hunting. I was a neophyte. You and my dad took me under your wings and taught me everything about the sport. Most days, I went with Dad, but sometimes I hunted with you. Everything I know about elk hunting I learned from the two of you. As much as I truly loved my real dad, I have considered you, for many years, as my second dad. Now that my real Dad has been elevated to higher headquarters, I just think of you as my Earthly dad." That was so very flattering; it made me feel good. I expressed my joy to Brett. However, I couldn't resist the temptation of a joke. I replied, "Brett, I am very honored. I gratefully accept the roll. However, when my will is read someday, don't be shocked if you hear the names Mary Lou, Randy and Robyn mentioned, but yours seems to be omitted. Love can only be stretched so far, Brett." We both laughed quite hearty.

However, with Brett's two future retirements; one as a Lt. Colonel from the Colorado Air Guard and one from United Airlines, we won't have to take up collection for him and his wonderful family. They should afford a hamburger or two!

It's time to go hunting! I boarded a Delta plane in Atlanta and flew to Denver with my trusty rifle, of course, with all the rest of my hunting gear and lots of warm clothes on the early morning flight of Oct. 8th. Why leave so soon since the season was four days away.

If you have ever spent much time in Colorado, then you know about the weather. It can change, often so dreadfully, in just a few hours. October 9th was reported to be a beautiful day, and it was. That would put us in the timber a day early, on Wednesday. If a sudden snowstorm comes, we will be ready. Also, by leaving early, we could ensure the rental of Pat Mantel's horses to transport all our gear into camp. We would walk in. By waiting, horses could become scarce, since competition builds rapidly as the season approaches. First come, first served, as the old saying goes.

My buddy, Brett Berringer, was at the Denver airport to pick me up. We spent the night at Brett's home with his darling wife Heidi, son Brayden, and daughter Hallie.

Brett and I departed for the high country very early the next morning. We met with Todd at Silverthorne, a town just north of I-70, to eat breakfast. We were also joined at the restaurant by a close friend of Todd and Brett. He, Willy-O, was driving his own pickup. I had never met him before, but he and his son Will were great company; very likable. He, being a retired Colonel, had once been Brett's boss. Obviously, he had treated Brett fairly or he would never have been invited to the camp. To hunt from our camp is an honor and a privilege! Both Willy-O and his son Will were a pleasure to know, camp, and hunt with.

With all three pickups, we drove to the Outfitter's station. There was Kevin, the same ranch foreman, hard at work as usual. We were so pleased to see each other again, as we discussed my last hunt three years earlier. Remember, it was Kevin who came and brought me back to his ranch, Sombrero, in 2016. Mary wasn't there when we arrived, but was there when we finished our hunt. We hugged profusely to reunite old friendships. During our warm embrace, I once glanced over at Kevin, hoping for his approval. I might not be too old to hunt, but I'm definitely too old to fight. Kevin had a wide grin of satisfaction on his face. We three will always be buddies.

Brett's son Brayden, and Will, the son of Willy-O drove up a day or two later to take advantage of school work, etc. Will, not as experienced with elk hunting yet, will hunt with his dad. Brayden, an old veteran now, with several bulls to his credit, will hunt alone.

Triston drove up to join us the following day. Todd and his son, Triston will hunt together. What year Triston is having! First of all, he will graduate from the Air Force Academy next June, becoming a Second Lieutenant and Air Force pilot. Just after his graduation, he will wed his beautiful sweetheart of many years. As if that isn't enough, Triston shot his first bull elk an hour before I shot my last one. So now you know. I went elk hunting again after promising to hang it up in 2016. Sorry, I just couldn't help myself. The "call of the wild" was beginning to beckon me again; what could I do? I needed #25. Will shot a nice bull the day after Triston and I shot ours on opening day.

Willy-O retired from the Colorado Air Guard as a colonel. What do you think he does now for a living? Yep, you guessed it; a United Airline pilot. Brett will join United Air Lines full time after his twenty- year Air Guard career on one October 2020.

The elk hunt of 2019 was definitely my last. I can't go back on my word this time, like I promised in 2016, after escaping near disaster in that dreadful snow storm on Oct. 18th and 19th. I promised not to return, and to leave that sport to the youth. After much training at the gym to remain in shape, I decided to give it another try. I had collected 24 bulls since 1972 and wanted #25 if possible.

I survived the hunt unscarred. Now, I'm so pleased I did. Lucky for me, there wasn't any deep snow this time; only light snow.

First rifle season in Colorado was October 12th through October 16th, 2019, but the entire extravaganza took much longer. We have always insisted on being all settled in camp with all work done on Thursday before the Saturday opening day each season.

We cut lots of firewood for our stove on Thursday; enough for the season and stack it in its customary place behind the stove. Happiness is being warm and cozy by a glowing stove while it is snowing so treacherously outside.

A couple of us will go to the stream that runs just thirty yards east of our tent and collect gallons of water for drinking and camp use such as washing dishes, etc. We make lots of Gatorade and cool aid for drinking. We don't make coffee in camp. It can make us hyper, and please, no alcohol. Hunting can be too stressful, particularly in bad weather, to allow any distraction. Besides, God is watching, and we need all the help we can muster.

On packing in to our campsite, everything ran smooth. Todd and I left early to walk the four miles into our camp. None of us knew (and certainly not them) how well this 81-year-old man could climb those steep mountain hills. I thought I could, but I even surprised myself. They didn't seem any harder than before. As we climbed, Todd asked me two or three times if he could carry my gun for me, feeling sorry for old Methuselah; (remember him from Genesis in your Bible; Noah's grandpa). I said, "Thank you very much Todd, but I can't let you. A hunter must climb with his own gun." We both reached camp shortly before Brett and Willy-O. Kevin and his men with horses arrived with all our gear very quickly thereafter.

We spent that afternoon and the next day, Thursday, putting up our tent (12 x 14 ft.), and rain shield as we erected all poles. Then we placed all our hunting clothes, sleeping bags, and all gear for each of us in its proper place. We arranged all food and liquid in its usual place; The Pantry.

Then on Friday we will relax and be quiet, so as not to disturb any elk that could be passing nearby. We also journey throughout the hunting region for miles each Friday afternoon to pick up any evidence of where the herd is located, especially where we think they will be bedding down for the night. Then we creep away, undetected hopefully, and return to camp to compare notes, and discuss where each of us plan on being at the crack of daylight the next opening morning; Saturday.

On Friday evening, the day before the start of the hunt, we were all nestled in, rested and comfortable. Now, all we must do is cook our supper, eat, wash dishes, and pack our lunches and water for the following day. Get to bed early, go to sleep, and rest well because 5 A.M. in the morning will come early and we will be ready. Excitement fills the air, as we try to sleep with a full stomach and high expectations. Now just close our eyes and doze off. Note: I have never been good at that part, especially the night before season opener.

On this hunt, just like all others, my plan was set. I would go alone to one of my favorite ridges to hunt, especially if I had seen evidence of recent elk activity on my Friday afternoon scouting.

Now, I don't want to accuse two fine camp leaders of having a secret conference to discuss the old man of the camp. Though I agree with them on their decision in afterthought. I have a suspicion that the subject was brought up about Jim Fogg being lost in that snowstorm in 2016 and never finding his way back to camp. (P.S. Brett went looking for me on that dreadful night – Bless his heart, as we say down South – and couldn't find his way back to camp either). His son Brayden and nephew, Matt, were able to guide Brett back safely to camp, with frequent rifle shots. I was too far away by then, for their shots to assist my returning to camp.

Neither Todd nor Brett wanted me to venture off too far and be lost again, even though the weather was good. They know me! It has been a few years since I climbed to the top of Pyramid Peak (over 12,000 ft. high), and I just may get a wild hair and climb to its summit to see if it has changed any.

Since Triston had never bagged a bull, Todd wanted to hunt with his son to improve his chances. I understand. I remember the joy of many years ago, hunting with my son, Randy.

Brett's son, Brayden, full of confidence now, no longer needs his dad's help. Therefore, Brett informed me that he would like to hunt with me on opening day. I was shocked at first, but thinking of making my last hunt, in quiet conversation with my pal and fellow elk hunting connoisseur, I began to like the idea. To tell you the truth, I enjoy conversation! I knew that Brett and I could venture out and maybe shoot a bull if one happened along our way. If he did, he had better be very crafty and quick to avoid the thunder of our two guns.

Once more as we would reminisce over those memorable yesteryears; of days long gone by in this basin, would be quite enjoyable for both of us. Brett was always very attentive as I recalled stories about his father, grandfather, and I, In pursuit of those gallant monsters in the 1970's before Brett became old enough to hunt.

Hunting was fun for both of us as we softly chatted all day of Oct 12th; opening day, and we did very little traveling. We could view the entire lower Eastern slope of

Quake Ridge without going far from camp. For all these years we have been climbing our favorite three ridges of Quake, Spur, and Main, up to 11,300 feet and ignoring the lower portion. Their thousands of tracks would prove that the elk very often passed by, even within twenty yards of our tent, while we were up very high looking for them.

Our tent sits at the lower tip of Spur Ridge, sandwiched between those two magnificent ridges of Main and Quake, where the elk travel every morning and afternoon as they proceed to and from their feeding meadow and their mid-day isolated seclusion. This is just one of their avenues of travel. They use at least a couple dozen more. We always hope to be at the right place at the right time.

At midday we chose what we thought would be a perfect spot to eat our lunch, and then spend the rest of the day casually talking and resting. From this one spot we could see the entire lower Eastern hillside of Quake Ridge. Brett loved it because he didn't want to tire the old man out. I loved it since we could rest and chat all afternoon. When it comes to elk presence, one spot is often just as good as another. We all have our favorites, of course, but this spot at the 9,400 feet level, near camp, seemed befitting for this day.

Just fifteen feet west of our new stand, runs one of the two streams that encircle our camp. Our stand was comprised of two large Quake trees (four feet apart) put there by the Lord so Brett and I could have a perfect view of the entire hillside, while resting our backs against as we chatted away.

At about 5:00 P.M., Brett and I heard one shot up high. That means that the elk must be moving already. Little did we know that shot was from Triston, shooting his first bull elk ever, from Buford's meadow. That stand has always been our favorite. I shot my first Royal bull from that same stand in 1992.

Neither Bill, nor Todd, nor Brett saw me shoot that bull, because they were one hundred- and -fifty yards up hill, around the corner and out of sight, skinning out a bull elk that Brett had shot two hours earlier. They clearly heard my shot and came running to check it out. This Royal was a beauty with six good points per side. Thus, we have two bulls to haul out from that day's hunt. Brett had shot his bull also, from Buford's stand in the middle of Buford's meadow; named because of our love for our first donkey who must get busy and transport both bulls out of the timber to our pickups, miles away at season's closure.

It can be uncanny sometimes how similar events occur. Brett Berringer shot his first bull elk on his first hunt at fourteen years old hunting with his Dad, Bill. I shot my first six- point (Royal) bull that same day of October, 1992, just after Brett shot his. Now, here in October 2019, Triston Berringer shot his first bull from the same stand, also hunting with his dad, Todd, just one hour before I would shoot my last one. What a stand!

Suddenly, at about 5:30 P.M. Brett said, "Look Jim, there is a cow coming over the ridge." I looked and saw that cow coming down, being followed by another cow. Both of these were about 150 yards away, traveling through the Quakes from our left to right as they were heading straight for the huge meadow below.

Within seconds another cow came down followed by two more cows; all three appearing from the same spot we had seen the first two. The herd is surely moving now. Things are heating up. These three, instead of following the first two cows, are coming straight down the hill toward us. We old hunters learned long ago to keep our eyes peeled to the same spot where we first saw the cows appear. If a bull is coming, he will be following about one or two hundred yards behind.

My buddy, Bill Berringer, learned this lesson the hard way on our third hunt. He loved to sit on his favorite rock, a large one, where he could scan that Western side of Main Ridge. A herd of cow elk passed below his stand. After they passed and there were none following close behind, Bill thought there were no more, so he stood up on his favorite rock. What bill didn't see was that trailing bull, but that bull surely saw Bill. That sly bull quickly detoured further down the hill out of Bill's sight. But that bull still wanted to rejoin his herd of cows. So, they later rejoined and came running swiftly around the point of Main Ridge, just below where I was sitting. I let the cows pass by with no notice of me. I waited only thirty seconds in a motionless state, and here comes that crafty bull in hot pursuit. I shot him in his lower neck, in his vertebrae and dropped him practically in his tracks.

Bill was so disgusted at his mistake. He would never make that error again, as he dropped very many bulls during the rest of his life. I don't recall Bill ever telling me his bull count, but his number was large also. Bill was one of the best all-around hunters I ever knew. He surely has two sons who, very likely, will surpass Bill and my record before they are through. Remember, "The apple never falls far from the tree." Also, they both started hunting at the age of fourteen. Maybe Bill and I were two "Dudes", as Pat Mantle called us on our first visit; but we sure learned fast and tried never to make the same mistake twice. We were both determined.

Please! Let's get back to Brett and I watching those cow elk coming down the hill at 5:30 P.M. on opening day. I kept my eyes drilled on the spot where I had first seen the cows, as I am sure Brett did likewise. All at once there appeared a very large set of horns coming over the hill, attached to a huge beautiful bull elk. Though I am sure Brett saw him also, I quickly said, "Look Brett, here comes the bull." He came straight down the hill toward us, following those last three cows. It didn't take Brett and I long to discover what that bull's focus was. We were the furthest thing from that bull's mind at that time.

Those three cows stopped and stood stone still at the edge of the clearing in front of Brett and I, just fifty yards away. There was not one tree in that small meadow. Only grass and weeds, giving us a perfectly unobstructed view.

It very soon became perfectly clear that this bull elk was enamored with the third cow, the one behind the other two. He came straight down and stopped just behind her. She, enjoying the chase, decided to tease him a bit more and traveled off about fifteen feet. This left him standing alone, broadside, very still, just fifty yards from us, without even a twig between us, and two rifle scopes perfectly trained on that bull's side. That bull never looked our way.

Brett and I sat motionless with our fingers on our rifle triggers, staring through our scopes. My rifle has two triggers. When the aft is pulled, it turns the front trigger into a hair trigger. Now I must only touch the front trigger and the bullet is on it's way. But we both sat there so enamored with the view of this magnificent beast. This bull belongs to either one of us.

Out of curiosity I looked over at Brett who has his eye trained through his scope, just enjoying the view of that bull's right side. I drop my rifle to my lap and whisper;

"Shoot him Brett." He takes his eye from his scope, looks over at me, then lowered his rifle to his lap and whispers back to me; "No, you take him Jim." Not wanting to get into an argument at a time such as this, with a dear friend, I oblige and raise my rifle again. Just as I do, that bull has a treat for Brett and I. We have heard thousands of bull elk bugles through these scores of years of hunting, and have seen them in video film, but have never seen one in action in the wild; certainly not this close.

This bull decided at that moment to emit the most beautiful sounding bugle I have ever heard. Raising his head very high to impress that teasing cow, he opened his mouth to expose his bugle teeth and screamed a high pitch bugle. What a beautiful loud sound.

I let that bull finish his bugle and gave him another five seconds before I touched the front trigger of my rifle. That 180 grain Hornady bullet was on its way. Wow, what a shell it is; the most lethal one I have ever used. It slammed into that bull's right side, exploded through both lungs, and drilled a large hole out of his opposite side, the left one.

The bull immediately lunged forward for about ten yards, then made a 180-degree U-turn to his right and ran just twenty yards away from us broadside, as he passed by. I could tell from the blood color that was flowing from the large hole on his left side, as he ran by, that it was a lung shot and announced it to Brett. We both knew that bull was finished, but just as he quartered away from us, Brett let him have another shot just inside of his left front shoulder. Brett said later that he just couldn't resist the temptation. Elk hunting is so very exciting!

That bull ran out of our sight, crossed the stream that ran in front of us about forty yards upstream, all obscured by the forest, and proceeded another fifty yards across the tip of Spur Ridge, our camp ridge. He succumbed a measured sixty-five yards above our tent up against a timber tree. How accommodating he was! Of our 121 bulls we have shot through the years, none have ever fallen so close to camp; none have ever been shot so close to camp.

Just why did this bull make it so easy for this old hunter to reach his #25? You tell me! I think my experience of my narrow escape in 2016 has changed me for good. I don't believe I shall ever be the same again. Though I can't see my Lord anymore since that fateful early morning of Oct. 19, 2016, I feel certain that I often feel his presence. What a gratifying feeling.

One thing is certain! After my Lord's revelation during my hunt in 2016, and my reward during this hunt of 2019, it is impossible for me to ever surpass these two hunts. Therefore, I am hanging up on elk hunting for good, and live, reflecting on all my hunts with those splendid Berringers and other much- loved relatives and friends. I remain contented and appreciative of all God's blessings through my loving Savior, for the remainder of my life.

My desire is that you, all your family and dear friends, receive peace and joy throughout your days on this Earth, then pass on to an existence far greater than anything we have ever experienced. Our Lord is patiently waiting for you.

A most sincere blessing to each of you, now and forever.

James R. Fogg Jr.

Jim Fogg, Descending Quqke Ridge
after a successful hunt

Left to right; Bill, J.B., Jim, Poss

Bill's oldest Son, Todd, and Jim

L to R, Bill's Twin Brother, Warren, their
Dad- Mr. Berringer, Jim, and Poss.

Jim's first bull; Rabbit Ears Pass.

L to R; J.B., Jim, Mr. Berringer, Bill

Jim's first bull, exactly where he fell at Jim's feet

L to R –Buford, Bill, Jim, Son Randy (13), J.B., Mr. B

Jim again, probably still shaking!

Brett (14); His first Bull

Three happy hunters: Todd, Bill, Jim

Bull elk #25 ; Jim & Brett

Jim Fogg in his office, among a lifetime of memories!
Jim is holding elk rack #25; elk rack #1 on the wall

Printed in the United States
by Baker & Taylor Publisher Services